Animal Habitats

The Squirrel in the Trees

Text by Jennifer Coldrey

Photographs by
Oxford Scientific Films

Gareth Stevens Publishing
Milwaukee

A wood like this is just the sort of place to find squirrels.

Tree-living squirrels around the world

Squirrels that live in the trees are common in many countries. They can be found in many different kinds of woodland and forest, as well as in the trees of parks and yards. Tree squirrels are well suited to their life in the trees. They are wonderful climbers, with long, bushy tails which help them to balance as they move. The word squirrel comes from the Greek meaning "shade-tail" or "shadow-tail." This explains how squirrels often use their tails, like parasols, to shade their bodies from the sun.

   Some squirrels, such as the American Grey Squirrel, like to live among broad-leaved trees such as oak, beech, walnut, and sycamore. Others, like many of the red squirrels, prefer to live among *coniferous* trees such as pine, spruce, and larch.

*A Grey Squirrel nibbles at the
leaves and buds on an oak tree.*

There are tree-living squirrels in tropical forests, too. In parts of Africa and Asia live tiny pygmy squirrels no bigger than mice, while in India and Malaya there are large, brightly-colored "giant" squirrels as big as cats. Flying squirrels are found in parts of Asia, Europe, and North America. These animals have two flaps of furry skin stretching between their front and back legs. These flaps open out like a parachute when the squirrel jumps, allowing it to glide through the air from tree to tree. Unlike other squirrels, flying squirrels are active only at night.

A British Red Squirrel is at home in this pine tree.

A Grey Squirrel eats an acorn which it has found on the woodland floor.

Home in the trees

Tree-living squirrels occasionally come down onto the ground where they scamper about, searching for food among the grass or fallen leaves. But their main home is up in the trees. Here they are safe from most enemies and it is here that they build their nests to sleep and find shelter in.

Squirrels sometimes nest in holes in tree trunks. They also build hollow, ball-shaped nests, made out of twigs and bark and lined with moss, grass, and dead leaves. These are called *dreys*. They are usually wedged between the branches and are quite easy to spot up in the trees, especially in winter, when many trees lose their leaves.

When you next walk through some trees, look up into the branches. If you are lucky you may see a squirrel climbing and leaping about in the treetops. If you move quietly, standing still to listen now and again, you may hear squirrels chattering and calling, as well as moving through the leaves and occasionally dropping nuts or pine cones onto the ground.

The trees provide a lot of food for squirrels, including nuts, seeds, fruit, buds, and shoots. You may find the scattered remains of their feeding on the ground under the trees. Look for the split shells or husks of nuts and seeds, as well as pine cones stripped of their scales and seeds. You may also notice nibbled toadstools, bulbs, and shoots dug up out of the ground, or bare patches on the tree trunks where squirrels have peeled off strips of bark to feed on the sap beneath. There are other signs to look out for, too, such as scratch marks on the smooth bark of trees where squirrels have been climbing, and foot prints in the mud or snow beneath the trees.

This squirrel's drey is wedged in a fork between the branches of an ash tree.

Look up into the trees and you may see a squirrel leaping through the branches.

The squirrel's body

Tree squirrels are attractive animals, with their long, bushy tails, sleek, silky fur, and beady black eyes. There are many different varieties throughout the world, but greyish-brown and brownish-red are some of the commonest.

The European Red Squirrel is found in Britain and in many parts of Europe and Asia. It has several color variations ranging from a pale gold to nearly black. The adult Red Squirrel is about 15½ inches (385mm) long from its nose to the tip of its tail and weighs about 10½ oz (300g). Its coat is a rich chestnut color which becomes much darker and greyer, as well as much thicker, in winter. The undersides are white. The Red Squirrel has very obvious tufts of hair on its ears which become especially thick in winter. In the British variety these turn a pale, creamy-white in summer and so does the tail.

The red squirrels of the North American pine and spruce forests are smaller than European Red Squirrels. They are noisy little animals and show a black line along their sides in summer. This is a Douglas Pine Squirrel, or Chickaree, from the western U.S.

A British Red Squirrel feeds on blackberries in the autumn.
Notice the tufts of hair on its ears.

The Grey Squirrel, pictured on page 4, comes from eastern parts of North America, although it is now common in Britain, too. It was introduced into Britain about one hundred years ago. It is larger and heavier than the British Red Squirrel, with a body measuring 18½ inches (470mm) from its nose to the tip of its tail. Its fur is greyish-brown with chestnut-colored markings on the head, down the middle of the back, and on its sides and paws. The undersides are white. In winter the coat and tail become much thicker and more silvery-grey. The Grey Squirrel has tufts on its ears only in the winter, but they are not nearly as obvious as those of the Red Squirrel.

A squirrel's plume-like tail is one of the most important parts of its body. It is used for steering and balancing up in the trees and acts as a sort of parachute when the animal leaps through the air. Squirrels also use their tails for keeping warm. When they curl up to sleep, they wrap their tails around themselves like a woolly scarf.

Squirrels have large eyes set on the sides of their heads, giving them good all-round vision. Good eyesight is very important for high-speed travel through the treetops. Squirrels can hear quite well, too, and will prick up their ears to listen for sounds nearby. They have an excellent sense of smell which is especially useful for finding food. Long black whiskers grow from their muzzles and from around their eyes and below their chins. These are sensitive to touch.

Squirrels are rodents, which means that they have long, sharp front teeth, called *incisors*, which they use for gnawing and cutting. The incisors never stop growing and could become dangerous, possibly piercing through the opposite jaw, if they were not worn down by regular use. Squirrels keep them trimmed by continually gnawing on nuts, bones, tree bark, and other hard things.

At the back of the mouth are the grinding teeth or *molars*. Between the incisors and the back teeth there is a large gap on each side of the jaw. This allows the squirrel to close off the back of its mouth by pinching in the skin on each side of the gap. When it nibbles on nuts, pine cones, or bark, the hard pieces drop out at the front of the mouth and are not swallowed.

The toes on a squirrel's feet are long and slender. They have sharp, curved claws which are very useful for gripping the bark of trees. The front paws, each with four toes, are also used for gathering and holding food. The longer and heavier back feet — each with five toes — are especially good at gripping and help the squirrel to balance when it is sitting. Squirrels often hang upside down to feed, clinging onto a branch with only their back feet.

Left: A Grey Squirrel sits on a fence post to eat a pea-pod. It grips the food in its front paws, while its back feet and tail help it to balance.

This close-up picture of a squirrel's nose and mouth shows the nostrils, the whiskers, and the long, cutting incisor teeth.

Movement

Squirrels move through the trees like acrobats. They have a wonderful sense of balance and can run along tiny branches and up and down tree trunks with astonishing speed and skill. They always come down a tree head-first, back feet turned out at right angles to the body, using their claws to cling onto the bark. Up in the treetops they leap about like trapeze artists, jumping from branch to branch, and even from tree to tree. Their strong back legs help them to leap distances of up to 12 feet (4m). When they jump, they flatten their bodies and fluff out the hairs on their tails to help them sail through the air more easily.

Flying squirrels can glide through the air for up to 60 yards (20m) or more, using the wing-like flaps of skin on either side of their bodies. Their flattened tails help them to steer, and they can change direction if necessary by tilting slightly to one side. Just before landing, they lift up their tails to help them brake and stretch their front legs upwards. They land on a tree trunk with all four feet gripping the bark, their flattened tails pressed against the trunk for support.

Squirrels move on the ground in little leaps or runs, holding their tails straight out behind them. They can move quite fast, bounding along at speeds of up to 20 miles per hour. Squirrels can swim quite well, too.

An American Fox Squirrel clings to the bark with outstretched feet as it runs down a tree trunk head-first.

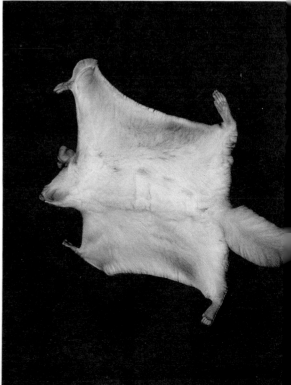

An American flying squirrel glides through the air with legs outstretched.

A squirrel holds a pine cone in its front paws while it bites off the scales to get at the seeds.

Food and feeding

Squirrels are mainly plant-eaters, and most of their food comes from the trees. They eat all kinds of nuts, including acorns, hazelnuts, walnuts, beechnuts, and chestnuts. They also eat many other woodland fruits and seeds, including rose hips, hawthorn berries, and blackberries. Red squirrels and others which live in coniferous woodland feed mainly on the seeds from pine, spruce, or larch cones.

Squirrels usually hold food in their front paws while nibbling at it with their teeth. They sometimes carry the food away in their mouth, to a safe place, before eating it. When feeding on the ground, they often have a favorite perch, maybe a tree stump or log, for eating. Squirrels have a clever way of opening hard-shelled nuts, such as hazelnuts, to get at the kernel. They first nibble a hole at the pointed end. Then they push their lower incisors into the shell, and use them like a crowbar to split the shell, lengthwise, into two halves.

Squirrels are also very skillful at getting at the tiny winged seeds tucked down between the scales of pine and spruce cones. Starting at the bottom of the cone, they bite off the scales one by one, picking out the seeds as they go, until the cone becomes stripped and bare. The scales and wings of the seeds, together with the central core, are left behind on the forest floor. Many birds, like woodpeckers and crossbills, also eat the seeds from pine cones, but they do not remove the scales. It takes a squirrel only a few minutes to strip and eat the 30-40 seeds in a pine cone, and one red squirrel can eat well over a hundred pine cones in a day.

All that remains of a pine cone eaten by a squirrel is the central core, stripped of its seeds and scales.

This Grey Squirrel has taken a piece of apple to a safe place up in the trees to eat.

Squirrels eat different things at different times of the year. In autumn, they fatten up on the many fruits, nuts, seeds, and berries to be found in the woods. They also steal fruit, such as apples, pears, plums, and cherries, from orchards. They like eating toadstools, too. In spring, their favorite foods are the catkins, young buds, and leafy shoots of trees. They also dig up plant roots and bulbs, such as bluebells and daffodils, at this time of the year.

Food is generally harder to find in summer, and this is when squirrels gnaw at the bark of young trees. They often tear off long strips of bark to feed on the sweet sappy wood beneath. Unfortunately this often damages and may even kill the trees. Squirrels are basically vegetarian, although they do eat insects, as well as the eggs, and even the nestlings, of birds. They sometimes eat soil, which contains plenty of useful minerals and *roughage*. Squirrels rarely drink, except in very hot weather. They get most of the water they need from their food and from dew.

Squirrels are well known for their habit of hiding and storing food. They do this especially in the autumn when food is plentiful. Nuts and pine cones are buried underground or hidden away in dreys, tree trunks and hollows. These hidden stores are useful during the winter, and also at other times of the year, when food is hard to find. But squirrels do not plan ahead deliberately. They seem to discover hidden food more by chance than by memory and usually rely on their sense of smell to find it. Many nuts or pine cones are left forgotten in the ground, where some eventually sprout into young tree seedlings. In this way, squirrels can be useful in helping to plant new trees.

Autumn is the time to hide away extra food. Here a Grey Squirrel buries some acorns underground.

In warm summer weather, squirrels bask in the sun by lying flat out on the branches of a tree.

Activities

Tree squirrels are out and about during the day and are especially active in the early hours of the morning and in the late afternoon. They are lively and energetic when awake, although on hot summer days they like to lie flat out on their bellies on a branch, basking in the sunshine. In the middle of the day squirrels usually retire to a secluded branch or to their dreys to rest. They also sleep in their nests at night and will stay there for protection in very wet, cold, or windy weather.

In cold and wintry weather, squirrels shelter in their cozy nests, which are sometimes in a tree hole.

A Grey Squirrel peers into a large tree hole which could provide the shelter for its winter home.

In winter squirrels spend much more time asleep, coming out to look for food mainly in the middle of the day. Although they put on a lot of weight during the autumn, laying down layers of fat to tide them over the winter, squirrels do NOT *hibernate*. They cannot survive for more than a few days without eating, and even in the harshest weather, they have to come out to search for food.

Squirrels build different kinds of dreys at different times of year. The winter dreys are larger, thicker and more cozy than the summer nests. Winter dreys are usually built near the main trunk and are firmly wedged between the branches to prevent them being blown down in high winds. Sometimes in winter several squirrels may live together and share the same drey or nesting hole. This is especially common among young family groups. But adult squirrels normally live on their own, and one squirrel usually has several different dreys in its *territory*.

Two squirrels chase after each other in the woods.

Behavior

Although each squirrel has its own home area, it does not guard it vigorously to keep other squirrels out, and the territory of one animal often overlaps with another. However, squirrels are known to make scent marks in special places by squirting urine onto patches of bark on the trees. These smells are no doubt noticed by other squirrels and probably help to keep rivals away. Scent marking may also be used to attract a mate, although this has not yet been proved.

Squirrels are clean animals. They continually wash and groom themselves, and this helps to keep their skin and fur free from *parasites* — such as fleas, ticks, and mites — which often carry diseases.

Squirrels often play and fight with each other. They chase each other up, down, and around the trees, chattering and screaming and sometimes biting one another's tails. They have many different calls, including a harsh angry "chucking" noise, as well as moaning, barking, purring, and teeth-chattering. Each of these sounds has its own special meaning which the squirrels use to communicate with each other and to show feelings of fear, anger, excitement, or pleasure. They also use signals such as tail-flicking and foot-stamping to express their feelings. A squirrel's tail is never still. It is the most expressive part of the animal and is constantly flicking and twitching.

Squirrels are nervous, lively, and inquisitive animals, with very acute senses. They are always on the alert and will often pause to sniff the air, with ears erect and listening, ready to dart away at the slightest hint of danger.

A Grey Squirrel pauses to sniff the air, its senses on the alert for signs of danger.

Starting a family

Some squirrels have two breeding seasons during a year and some have only one. In Britain, both the Grey and most Red Squirrels produce their young at two different times of the year, once in early spring and again in mid-summer. However, a harsh winter can delay the spring breeding season. And if there has been a poor crop of nuts or pine cones the previous autumn, the breeding may be badly affected, so that only one summer family is produced the following year. This is because the females have not been able to put on enough weight to produce and feed babies in the spring.

During courtship the males chase the females through the trees with a lot of noisy chattering. Several males will chase after one female, until she suddenly stops. Then the first male to reach her is allowed to mate.

A female squirrel collects grass to line her nesting drey.

Newly-born squirrels are pink and hair-less, and their eyes and ears are closed.

Once pregnant, the female starts to make a nest for her family. She may build a new drey, repair and enlarge an existing one, or use a hole in a tree trunk. She lines the nest with moss, grass, and possibly sheep's wool or feathers, to make a soft, warm bed for her babies. She chases other squirrels, including her mate, away from the nest. The father is never allowed into the nesting drey, and he plays no part in rearing the young.

The young squirrels are born about six weeks after mating. There are usually three or four in a litter. They are pink and hairless when born and are unable to see or hear. Each kitten (as they are called) weighs only ½ ounce (15g) and measures about 4 inches (10cm) from its nose to the tip of its tail.

The mother looks after her babies well, keeping them warm and feeding them with her milk. She also licks and cleans them regularly. After about seven to ten days a thin down of hair appears and this becomes a thick coat by the time they are three weeks old. At about this time their teeth start to push through. Their eyes and ears open between four and five weeks, and the babies can then see and hear.

19

Growing up

If danger threatens, female squirrels sometimes move their babies to another drey. The mother picks up her babies one by one, gripping them in her mouth by the loose skin of their bellies. The baby curls its body around her neck and clings tightly with its claws. Baby squirrels have a very strong instinct to cling. This is important for any baby animal born up in the trees, as it helps to save them from falling.

At about seven weeks, the mother starts to bring her babies solid food, although she continues to suckle them until they are ten weeks old. By this time all their teeth are through and they become fully *weaned*. The young squirrels now start to explore the world outside the nest and to search for their own food. They soon learn to climb, and they will play and tumble around together, strengthening and exercising their muscles. The young also learn how to behave with other squirrels and how best to escape from danger.

They become completely independent by the time they are four months old. Some wander away and build dreys of their own to live in. Others stay in the area and return to their nesting drey to sleep and find shelter.

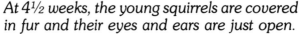

At 4½ weeks, the young squirrels are covered in fur and their eyes and ears are just open.

These young squirrels are exploring a bird box in the beech trees near their home.

By autumn there are lots of young squirrels about, and a forest may become overcrowded. At this time of year many squirrels, especially youngsters, move away to find other places to live. Many die during their first winter, from causes such as cold, starvation, disease, and accidents, as well as being killed by *predators*. The ones that survive can live for up to five or six years in the wild.

Young squirrels become fully grown at about six or seven months and are able to breed before they are a year old. One-year-old females only have one family in their first year.

Buzzards are birds of prey which nest in trees and occasionally pounce on squirrels in forests.

Natural enemies and ways of escape

Squirrels have very few natural enemies when they are up in the trees. Here they can escape from most dangers by leaping through the branches or darting into a tree hole. Their nests and young are also safely out of reach from most predators on the ground. However, birds of *prey* such as eagles, hawks, and buzzards sometimes catch them in the trees, and flying squirrels, which are active at night, are often preyed upon by owls.

Squirrels also have enemies that can climb the trees to hunt them. These include snakes, stoats, and weasels, wild and domestic cats, and animals called martens, which are members of the weasel family. Martens are much larger than weasels, with longer legs and big bushy tails. They live in trees and are expert climbers, well able to chase and catch a squirrel as it dashes through the treetops.

A Pine Marten stalks its prey across the snow.

But squirrels are in much more danger on the ground than they are up in the trees. They are easier to see and chase on the ground and may be pounced upon by a bird of prey, or hunted by foxes and dogs, as well as by snakes, stoats, weasels, and cats. Young squirrels are especially at risk as they are less experienced and less aware of danger than adults.

A squirrel's sharp, alert senses help it to avoid danger. When feeding on the ground, squirrels usually sit on a high perch, a tree stump, or a fence post, so that they can keep a look-out for enemies. When alarmed, they often stay completely still, as though frozen into position, so that a predator is less likely to see them. Their brown, grey, or reddish coloring blends in well with their surroundings, and this makes them difficult to see until they move.

A weasel looks up into the trees. Weasels and stoats climb up trees to chase squirrels and sometimes attack young squirrels in the nest.

Here a gamekeeper sets down a cage-trap in the wood for catching squirrels.

Humans and other dangers

Human beings also play a part in killing squirrels. This is mainly because these attractive little animals cause a lot of damage to trees. Sometimes they become a pest in woodland and forestry plantations, and when this happens, their numbers have to be controlled. People kill squirrels in various ways — either by shooting, snaring, trapping, or poisoning them. Sometimes, in the breeding season, the dreys containing females and young are poked out of the trees by men with long poles, and the squirrels are then shot or set upon by dogs.

People also harm squirrels when they cut down large numbers of trees and destroy their woodland *habitat*. This happened in Scotland during the 18th century, as more and more pine forests were cut down to make way for crops and grass to feed the sheep. As a result, the Red Squirrels had nowhere to live and nearly became *extinct* in parts of Scotland. Fortunately, more Red Squirrels were later introduced from England and new pine trees planted, so that Red Squirrels are still alive in Scotland today.

A Grey Squirrel is caught in a cage-trap. The animal is tempted into the trap by food such as corn or wheat.

In parts of Europe, Asia, and North America, people hunt squirrels for sport and also to provide them with food and fur. In Britain, squirrel fur is used to make paintbrushes and trout flies for fishermen, while in some parts of the country, gypsies and other country folk still eat squirrel pie.

Apart from all these dangers, squirrels die from other causes, too. In a hard winter many die from cold and hunger. Some are killed by accidents such as forest fires, by trees falling over, or when dreys with young are blown out of the branches in high winds. Squirrels also suffer from various diseases, some of which can kill them.

People damage and destroy the woodland habitat when they cut down large numbers of trees.

Squirrels as pests

Squirrels can cause a great deal of damage to the trees in forestry plantations. Their worst habit is bark-stripping. This is usually done on the main trunk, and if the squirrels remove the bark in a ring around the tree, the upper parts, and often the whole tree, will die. The bare patches make it easier for insect pests and fungus diseases to get in and damage the timber, and the trees later become scarred and deformed in their growth.

Squirrels cause further harm in the spring by biting off the buds and tender tips of the branches of young trees. This often spoils the future shape of a tree and makes it grow in a distorted way.

This tree has been badly damaged by squirrels which have stripped off the bark from the bottom of the trunk.

A Grey Squirrel peels off the bark of this sycamore tree to feed on the sweet sap beneath.

Grey Squirrels are bold enough to come into the yard and take food from a bird feeder.

Altogether, it is not surprising that squirrels are disliked by landowners and foresters. Gamekeepers do not like them either, because they eat the eggs and young of gamebirds, such as pheasants and partridges. Red squirrels become a pest mainly in coniferous forests, while Grey Squirrels cause a lot of serious damage to broad-leaved trees such as oak, beech, and sycamore.

Squirrels can also be a nuisance in gardens, fields, and orchards, where they come to eat the crops and sometimes damage the trees. Grey Squirrels are much less afraid of people than red squirrels are. They are often seen in town parks and yards, and will come to steal food from bird feeders. Some Grey Squirrels are so tame they will let people feed them by hand.

The Hazel Dormouse, found in parts of England and Europe, is chestnut brown and not much bigger than a mouse. Like most dormice, it is an agile climber.

Friends and neighbors

Squirrels share their home in the trees with many other animals. Birds are among their commonest neighbors and include owls, jays, woodpeckers, crows, and magpies, as well as many smaller birds. Squirrels and birds are usually quite good friends, unless a squirrel tries to steal a bird's eggs or young. The only way the birds can fight back is by ganging together and mobbing the squirrel. Squirrels sometimes use the abandoned nests of crows or magpies to make their dreys. They may also use an old woodpecker's hole for a den.

Apart from bats, very few *mammals* live in trees, except in tropical forests. But in some of the woodlands of Europe, Asia, and Africa, live some furry animals, rather like squirrels, called dormice. Dormice are smaller than squirrels, with very large eyes and long, usually bushy tails. Unlike squirrels, they sleep during the day and come out only at night to feed and play. They also hibernate during the winter.

The nuthatch is a familiar woodland bird. The adults are expert at hammering open nuts to eat, but the youngsters need to be fed on juicy insects and caterpillars.

Many other small mammals, including mice, voles, and shrews, live on the forest floor, while foxes, raccoons, badgers, and deer commonly make their homes in woodland. In North America and parts of Asia, chipmunks, which are also members of the squirrel family, often scamper up and down the trees collecting food. In tropical forests, many strange and extraordinary creatures live among the trees, including monkeys, snakes, sloths, parrots, and tree-frogs.

Many woodland animals eat the same kind of food as squirrels do. Mice, voles, dormice, chipmunks, and birds — such as woodpeckers, nuthatches, jays, and nutcrackers — can tackle nuts; while mice and various birds — including finches, crossbills, and woodpeckers — feed on pine-cone seeds. Deer, rabbits, and hares also nibble at the bark and young shoots of trees.

This Golden Mantled Ground Squirrel sometimes climbs trees to find food.

Life in the trees

Sometimes different kinds of squirrels live together in the same piece of woodland. In tropical forests, different kinds of tree squirrels live at different levels in the trees. This means they do not have to fight over the same food. In England, Red and Grey Squirrels sometimes live together in the same patch of mixed woodland. They may compete with each other for food, and when this happens, the Greys are usually more successful than the Reds. Grey Squirrels are larger, stronger, and apparently healthier than Red Squirrels. They seem to settle down more easily when they move into new areas of woodland, but it is not true that they attack and drive Red Squirrels out deliberately.

Most of the food that squirrels eat comes from the trees or from their woodland habitat. Squirrels in their turn are eaten by predators that live and hunt among the trees. If we draw a diagram we can see how squirrels form a link in the food chains between various plants and animals.

Food chain

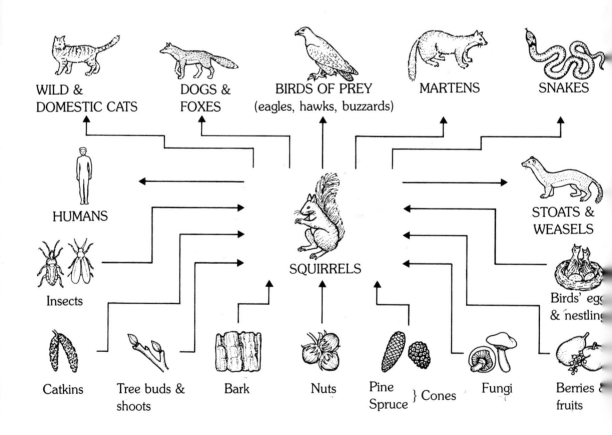

WILD & DOMESTIC CATS

DOGS & FOXES

BIRDS OF PREY (eagles, hawks, buzzards)

MARTENS

SNAKES

HUMANS

STOATS & WEASELS

Insects

SQUIRRELS

Birds' egg & nestling

Catkins

Tree buds & shoots

Bark

Nuts

Pine Spruce } Cones

Fungi

Berries & fruits

The squirrel, with its bushy tail, is undoubtedly one of the most lively and attractive animals to be found among the trees.

Tree squirrels are agile and sure-footed and very well adapted for their life in the trees. Here they can find food and shelter, as well as safety from many enemies. The North American (Eastern) Grey Squirrel is undoubtedly one of the most successful of all tree squirrels. It can survive in many of the habitats created by humans, and often lives close to people, in wooded areas of farmland and in town parks and yards. Most other tree squirrels are not as tame or so adaptable. They need quiet, undisturbed places to live. So it is very important that we keep plenty of large areas of wild, unspoiled woodland and forest, in which squirrels and other woodland creatures can survive.

Glossary and Index

These new words about squirrels appear in the text on the pages shown after each definition. Each new word first appears in the text in *italics*, just as it appears here.

coniferous .....cone-bearing (trees) with needle-like leaves, such as pine, spruce, and larch. **2, 11, 27**

drey ....a squirrel's nest in the trees, made out of twigs and leaves. **4, 13, 14, 15, 18, 19, 20, 24, 25**

extinct ....no longer existing. **24**

habitat ....the natural home of any plant or animal. **24, 25, 30, 31**

hibernate ......to spend the winter asleep. **15, 28**

incisors ....long, sharp cutting teeth at the front of a squirrel's mouth. **9, 11**

mammals .....animals with hair or fur which feed their young on milk. Squirrels, cats, and humans are mammals. **28**

molars ....back teeth which are used for crushing and grinding food. **9**

parasite ....an animal or plant that lives and feeds on another. **16**

predator ....an animal that kills and eats other animals. **21, 22, 23, 30**

prey ....an animal that is hunted and killed by another for food. **22, 23**

roughage ......coarse, indigestible matter in food, which is useful for keeping the bowels in good working order. **12**

territory ....piece of land which an animal defends against intruders. **15, 16**

weaned ....(of young animals) -- no longer dependent on their mother's milk for food, but now able to eat other things. **20**

Reading level analysis: SPACHE 4.2, FRY 4, FLESCH 87 (easy), RAYGOR 5, FOG 6, SMOG 3

Library of Congress Cataloging-in-Publication Data
Coldrey, Jennifer.
The squirrel in the trees.

(Animal habitats)
Summary: Text and photographs depict squirrels feeding, breeding, and defending themselves in their natural habitats.
1. Squirrels -- Juvenile literature. [1. Squirrels] I. Oxford Sceintific Films. II. Title. III. Series.
QL737.R68C65 1986   599.32'32   85-30292

ISBN 1-55532-087-2
ISBN 1-55532-062-7 (lib. bdg.)

North American edition first published in 1986 by
Gareth Stevens, Inc.
7221 West Green Tree Road Milwaukee, Wisconsin 53223, USA
Text copyright © 1986 by Oxford Scientific Films.

Conceived, designed, and produced by Belitha Press Ltd., London.
Typeset by Ries Graphics ltd., Milwaukee.
Printed in Hong Kong by South China Printing Co.
Series Editor: Jennifer Coldrey.
US Editors: MaryLee Knowlton & Mark J. Sachner.
Design: Treld Bicknell. Line Drawings: Lorna Turpin.
Scientific Consultants: Gwynne Vevers and David Saintsing.

The publishers wish to thank the following for permission to reproduce copyright material: **Oxford Scientific Films Ltd.** for pp. 1, 9, 11 below, 14 below, and 16 (photographer G.I. Bernard), pp. 3 above, 14 above, 15, 18, 21, 24, and 26 left and right (photographer John Paling), p. 2 (photographer David Thompson), p. 5 left (photographer G.A. MacLean), pp. 3 below and 7 (photographer D.J. Saunders), p. 11 above (photographer Godfrey Merlen), p. 12 (photographer Peter O'Toole), p. 13 (photographer Dave Houghton), p. 25 below (photographer Raymond Blythe), pp. 22 above and 29 (photographer M.P.L. Fogden), pp. 16, 23, 28 above, and 31 (Press-Tige Pictures); British Natural History Pictures for pp. 4, 5 right, 8, 25 above, and 28 below (photographer John Robinson); Survival Anglia for pp. 6 and 10 left (photographer Jeff Foott), p. 22 below (photographer Michael Strobino), and pp. 19 and 27 (photographers Liz and Tony Bomford); The Frank Lane Picture Agency for pp. 10 right and 20 (photographer Steve Maslowski). Front cover photographer: Dave Houghton. Back cover photographer: John Paling.